SPACE SHUTTLES

IAN GRAHAM

© Aladdin Books Ltd 1989

Designed and produced by
Aladdin Books Ltd
70 Old Compton Street
London W1

*First published in the
United States in 1989 by
Gloucester Press
387 Park Avenue South
New York, NY 10016*

ISBN 0-531-17172-8

*Library of Congress Catalog
Card Number: 89-50453*

Design David West
Children's Book Design

Editorial Lionheart Books

Researcher Cecilia Weston-Baker

Illustrator Ron Hayward
Associates

Printed in Belgium

CONTENTS

HOW · IT · WORKS
SPACE SHUTTLES

IAN GRAHAM

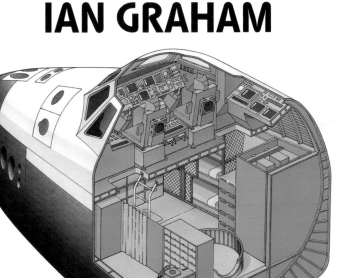

GLOUCESTER PRESS

New · York · London · Toronto · Sydney

THE WORKING PARTS

A Space Shuttle is a rocket-powered craft used to transport people, satellites and scientific experiments between the Earth and space. To do this, it must be able to fly in the Earth's atmosphere and in space. Unlike most rockets, which are used only once, a Space Shuttle is reusable. It can be used for many missions.

Shown here is the aircraft-like Orbiter, part of the United States' Space Shuttle. It has a large storage area, the payload bay, measuring 18 m (60 ft) long by 4.5 m (14 ft) wide for carrying cargo.

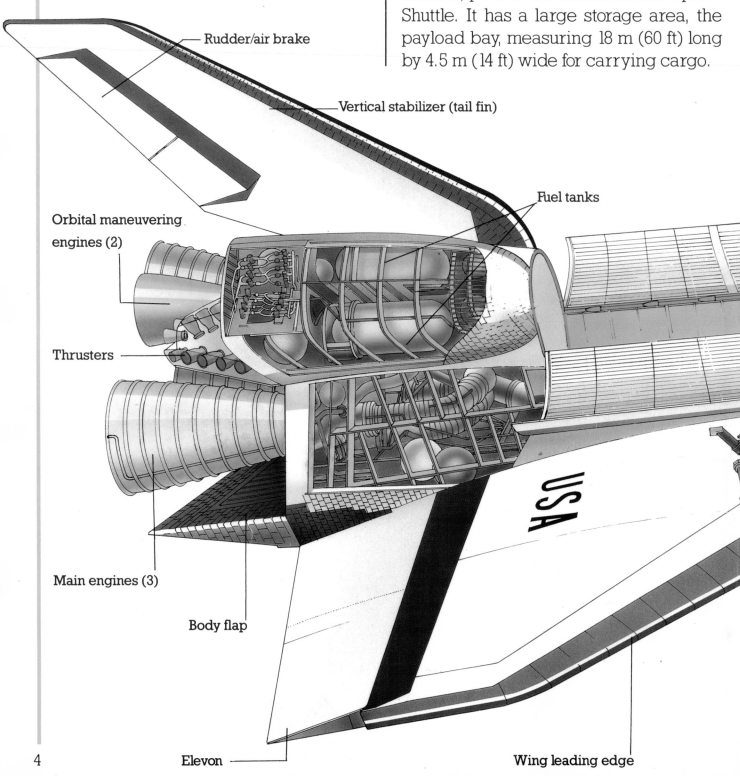

Rudder/air brake

Vertical stabilizer (tail fin)

Fuel tanks

Orbital maneuvering engines (2)

Thrusters

Main engines (3)

Body flap

Elevon

Wing leading edge

USA

When the payload bay doors are opened, radiators inside them help to cool the Orbiter by allowing heat to flow from them into space. A robot arm is used to move objects into or out of the payload bay.

In front of this bay is the crew compartment, where the astronauts live and work. The tail of the Orbiter houses five rocket engines. Three of them, called Space Shuttle Main Engines (SSMEs), are the most advanced liquid-fueled rocket engines ever built. Their nozzles can be turned to steer the craft and their power can be varied to control the Orbiter's speed. The SSMEs

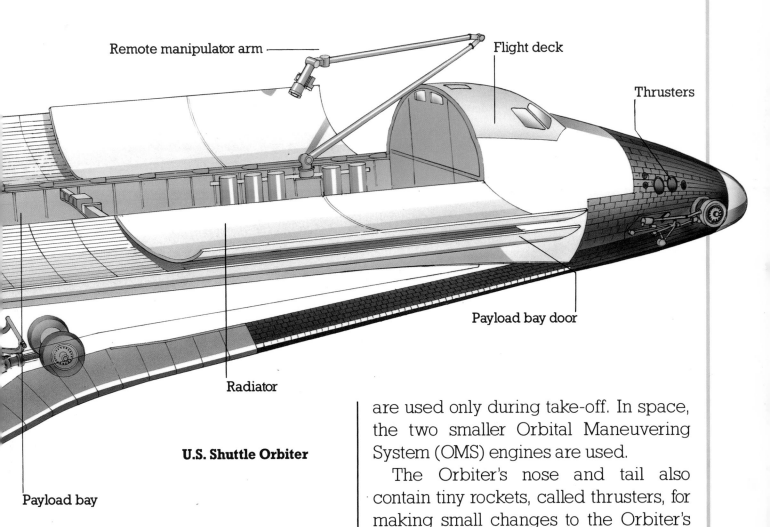

Remote manipulator arm

Flight deck

Thrusters

Payload bay door

Radiator

U.S. Shuttle Orbiter

Payload bay

are used only during take-off. In space, the two smaller Orbital Maneuvering System (OMS) engines are used.

The Orbiter's nose and tail also contain tiny rockets, called thrusters, for making small changes to the Orbiter's position. The Orbiter's wings have movable flaps called elevons. These, together with the body flap beneath the engines and the rudder, enable the Orbiter to maneuver when it re-enters the atmosphere before landing.

DIFFERENT TYPES

There are many different designs for a Space Shuttle. The most familiar is that used by the United States. The Soviet Union later designed a similar craft, but other countries have suggested alternative plans. All Shuttles need powerful rockets to overcome the Earth's pull of gravity on the craft.

Europe is building a Shuttle Orbiter called Hermes. It will be launched on top of a rocket. Hermes will be reusable, but not the rocket. West Germany plans to build its own Shuttle called Sanger. Its Orbiter will sit on the back of a powerful booster-craft and the two craft will take off together like an airplane.

The United States is already designing its next Space Shuttle, which it has named an airspaceplane. Using advanced construction materials and engines, it will fly to orbit at 12,500 km/h without the need for any add-on rockets or booster-craft. This craft is unlikely to be built before the year 2000.

The American Space Shuttle – the world's first reusable spacecraft

The Soviet Shuttle about to be launched

Europe's small Shuttle-craft, Hermes

A model of Britain's spaceplane

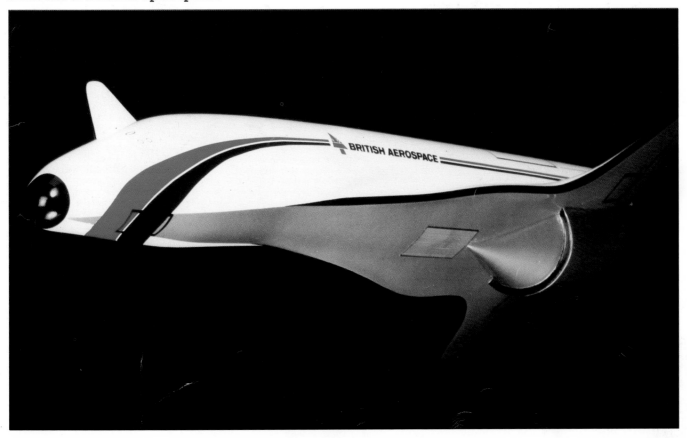

The U.S. Shuttle is carried to its launch site. The used SRBs fall away from the craft.

The outline of a typical Space Shuttle flight is shown below. On average, a flight lasts for about 7 days, although flights of up to 30 days are possible.

The Orbiter is propelled into orbit by its orbital maneuvering engines

The external tank is discarded when it is almost empty

Orbital operations (such as launching a satellite) take place

The solid rocket boosters are discarded at a height of about 45 kilometres

The tank breaks up in the atmosphere and falls into the ocean

The Space Shuttle is launched with three main engines and two rocket boosters

The boosters parachute down to the sea and are picked up by ship

THE REUSABLE CRAFT

Before the U.S. Space Shuttle came into service in 1981, astronauts and satellites were launched by rockets that were used only once and then scrapped. A different type of launcher was needed for a new Space Transportation System (STS). It would be a mixture of aircraft and spacecraft that could be used many times. The result is the Space Shuttle.

The Shuttle has three parts - the Orbiter, the Solid Rocket Boosters (SRBs) and the external fuel tank. After its work in space, the Orbiter returns to Earth and is used again. The two SRBs are also used again. When their job is finished, they parachute into the sea where they are collected by ship and used on a future flight.

The external fuel tank is not reusable. It is destroyed when it is dropped into the atmosphere during take-off to burn up or fall into the ocean.

Each Space Shuttle Orbiter should be capable of flying on 100 missions. The SRBs are designed to last for about 20 flights each. The precise lifetime and the number of flights an Orbiter or SRB is used for depends on the results of tests carried out after each flight.

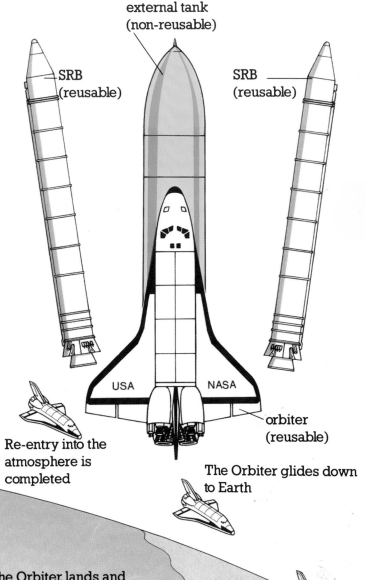

external tank
(non-reusable)

SRB
(reusable)

SRB
(reusable)

USA   NASA

orbiter
(reusable)

The Orbiter turns around and fires its orbital engines to slow down

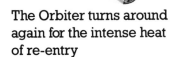

The Orbiter turns around again for the intense heat of re-entry

Re-entry into the atmosphere is completed

The Orbiter glides down to Earth

The Orbiter lands and the process begins again

TAKE-OFF

The events leading up to a Space Shuttle launch happen according to a timetable called the countdown. The final part of the countdown begins 5 hours before take-off, or at T minus (T−)5:00:00, when technicians go onboard the Orbiter and make sure that all its hundreds of switches are set correctly. At T−4:30:00, filling of the external fuel tank with hydrogen and oxygen begins.

The crew enters the Orbiter at T−1:50:00 and checks its systems, such as communications and guidance. The countdown clock is stopped several times before take-off for a few minutes

(longer if necessary), to allow for any unexpected problems to be dealt with. These stops are called "holds." The final planned hold, of 10 minutes, starts at 19 minutes before take-off.

Three seconds before take-off (T−0:00:03), the three main engines are ignited. If the Orbiter's computers detect any faults, the engines can be shut down. If all is well, the two SRBs are fired. Once the SRBs fire, the Shuttle must take off. Clamps holding the craft down and keeping it steady are released and it lifts off the launchpad with tremendous force and noise.

A U.S. Space Shuttle launch (left) is controlled by the Kennedy Space Center at Cape Canaveral, Florida. When the Shuttle rises above the launch tower, less than 7 seconds after lift-off, "Mission Control" at the Johnson Space Center in Texas (above) takes over. It keeps constant links with the astronauts.

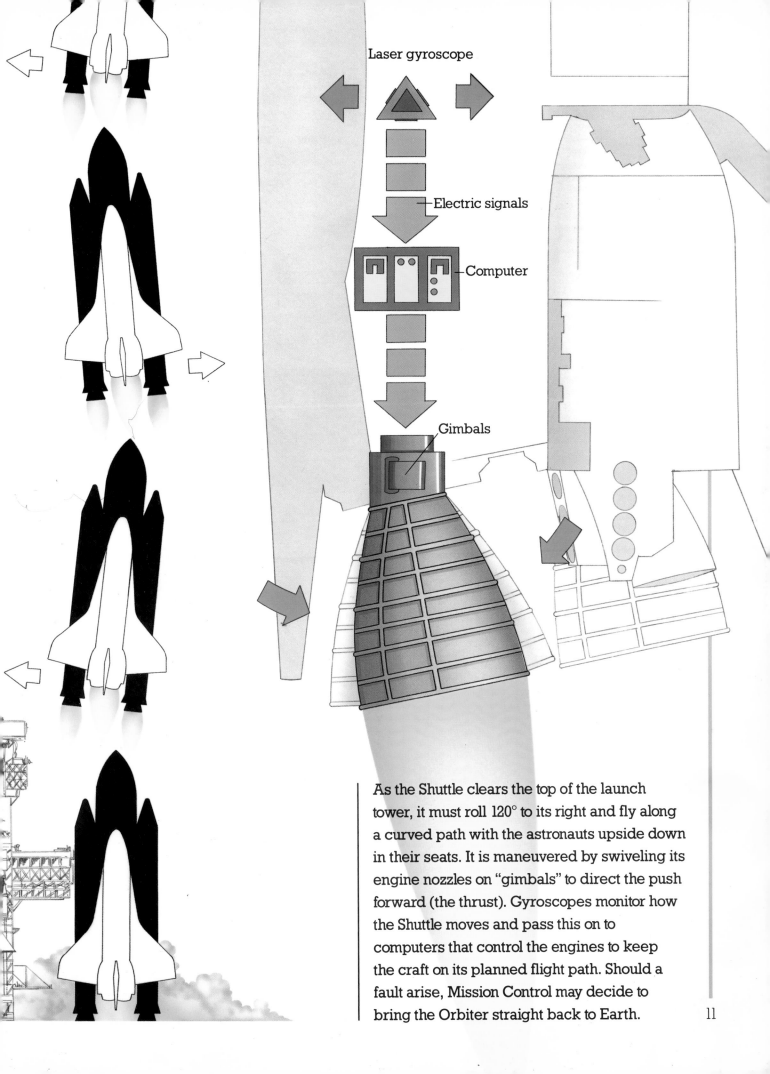

Laser gyroscope

Electric signals

Computer

Gimbals

As the Shuttle clears the top of the launch tower, it must roll 120° to its right and fly along a curved path with the astronauts upside down in their seats. It is maneuvered by swiveling its engine nozzles on "gimbals" to direct the push forward (the thrust). Gyroscopes monitor how the Shuttle moves and pass this on to computers that control the engines to keep the craft on its planned flight path. Should a fault arise, Mission Control may decide to bring the Orbiter straight back to Earth.

11

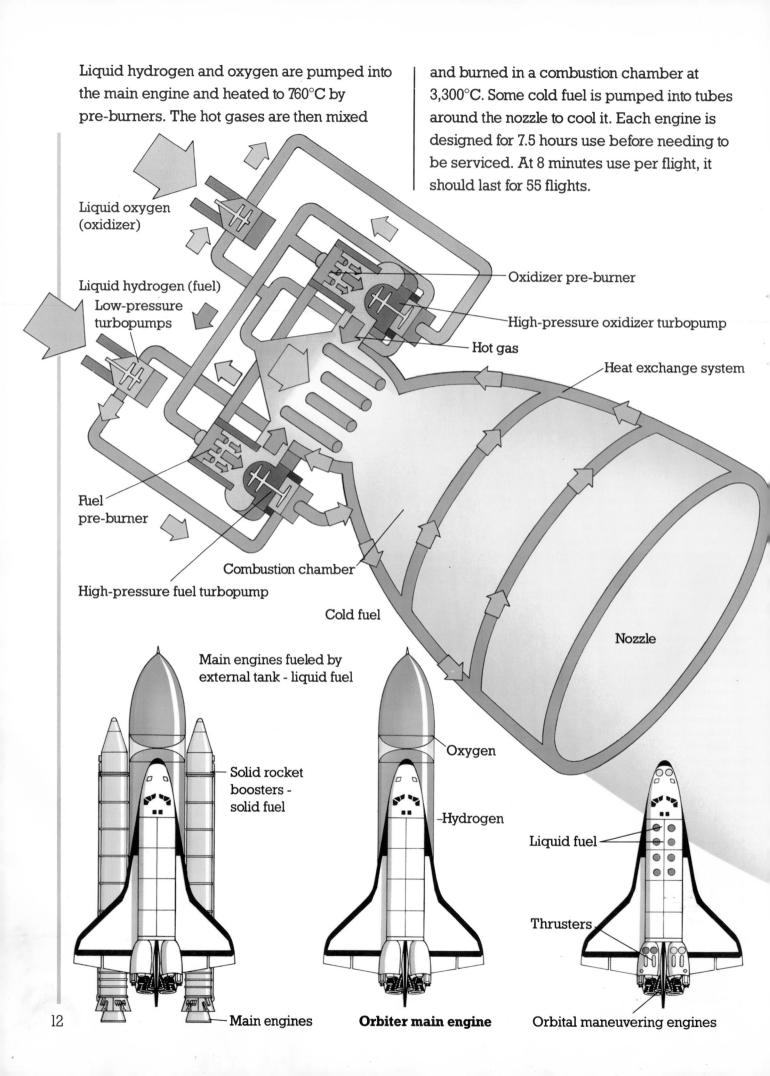

Liquid hydrogen and oxygen are pumped into the main engine and heated to 760°C by pre-burners. The hot gases are then mixed and burned in a combustion chamber at 3,300°C. Some cold fuel is pumped into tubes around the nozzle to cool it. Each engine is designed for 7.5 hours use before needing to be serviced. At 8 minutes use per flight, it should last for 55 flights.

Liquid oxygen (oxidizer)

Liquid hydrogen (fuel)

Low-pressure turbopumps

Oxidizer pre-burner

High-pressure oxidizer turbopump

Hot gas

Heat exchange system

Fuel pre-burner

High-pressure fuel turbopump

Combustion chamber

Cold fuel

Nozzle

Main engines fueled by external tank - liquid fuel

Solid rocket boosters - solid fuel

Oxygen

Hydrogen

Liquid fuel

Thrusters

Main engines

Orbiter main engine

Orbital maneuvering engines

CREATING THE POWER

The Space Shuttle's engines work by burning a fuel mixed with an oxidizer. The oxidizer provides oxygen which is essential for burning. (The oxidizer may be oxygen itself.) The fuel and oxidizer mixture is known as the propellant.

The Orbiter's main engines burn hydrogen fuel and oxygen pumped from containers in the external tank at over 300,000 liters per minute. The hot gases produced by burning the propellant rush out of the engines' nozzles, which can be swiveled to help steer the Shuttle. The engine power can be varied to control the Shuttle's speed. Each engine produces thrust capable of lifting a 170,000 kg (370,000lb) weight.

Each of the two booster rockets is a 45 m (148 ft) long tube packed with solid propellant, mainly a mixture of aluminum powder fuel and an oxidizer, ammonium perchlorate. Once each booster is ignited, it cannot be turned off. It burns until its fuel is used up. It produces 1.4 million kilograms of thrust.

In only 2 minutes, each solid-fuel rocket booster (right) consumes all of its 500,000kg of propellant to help the Shuttle take off. When the Orbiter is in space, it uses 2 liquid-fueled engines, the orbital maneuvering engines, to change its orbit and 44 tiny rocket motors, the thrusters (left), to make fine adjustments to its position. The thrusters are arranged in three groups – on the Orbiter's nose and on either side of its tail. When these are switched on, they sound like antitank shells being fired, as they send out huge tongues of flame. They have sufficient fuel to last the whole space voyage.

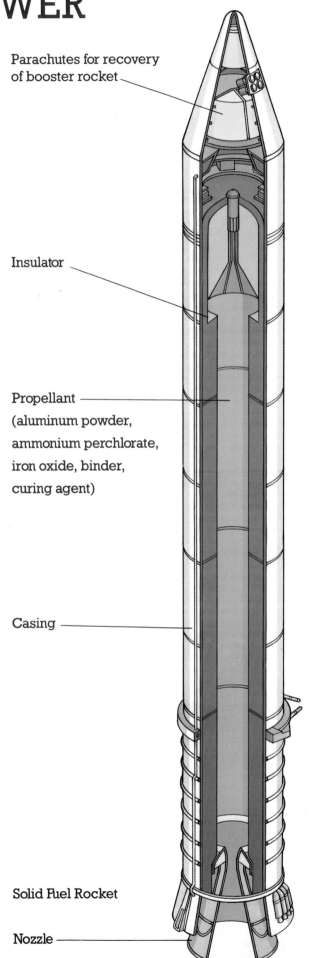

Parachutes for recovery of booster rocket

Insulator

Propellant (aluminum powder, ammonium perchlorate, iron oxide, binder, curing agent)

Casing

Solid Fuel Rocket

Nozzle

IN ORBIT

While the Shuttle is in orbit, it provides an Earth-like atmosphere for the crew members. They do not need to wear spacesuits. Instead they wear a loose-fitting jacket, shirt and pants.

The Orbiter has a small galley with an oven for preparing food. The astronauts sleep inside bags called sleep restraints to keep them from floating around in gravity-free space! The Orbiter has four beds, or sleep stations. Three are horizontal and one vertical, but as the astronauts are weightless, they are not aware of their orientation. Only four beds are needed because not all of the crew (of up to seven) will rest at the same time. Of course the Orbiter has a toilet. Unlike a toilet on Earth, the Orbiter's has handles and foot straps to keep an astronaut from floating off it!

Electrical power for the Orbiter is made by combining oxygen and hydrogen in fuel cells. A byproduct of this chemical reaction is water. This is used for drinking, washing, preparing food and cooling the cabin. About 3 kg (7lb) of water is produced every hour; up to 150 kg (330lb) can be stored in tanks. Excess water is dumped in space via outlet valves.

Secure in a sleep station on board the Orbiter

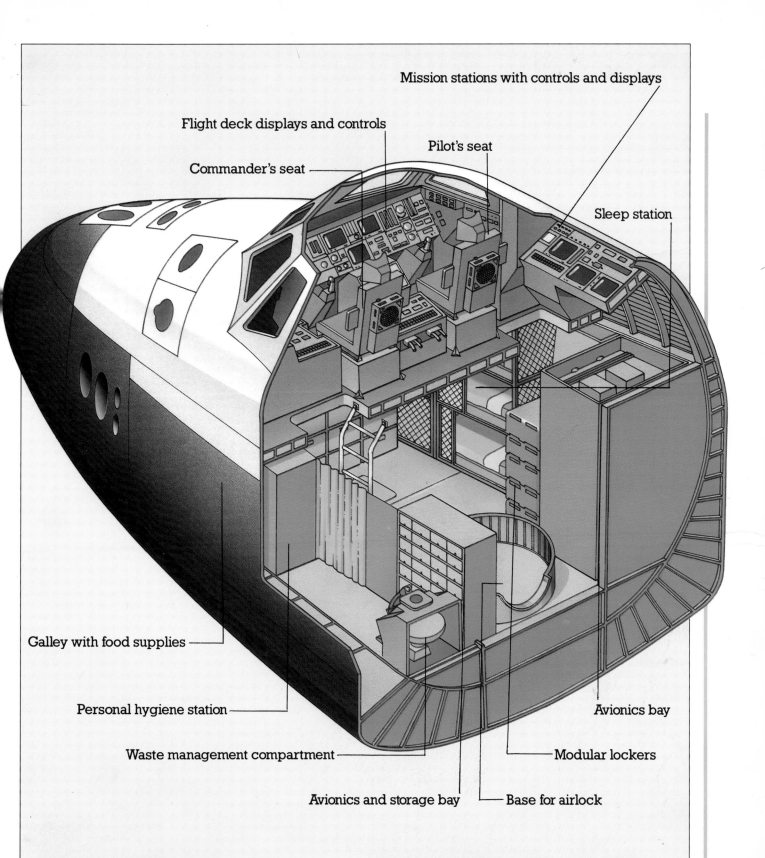

Mission stations with controls and displays

Flight deck displays and controls

Pilot's seat

Commander's seat

Sleep station

Galley with food supplies

Personal hygiene station

Waste management compartment

Avionics and storage bay

Base for airlock

Modular lockers

Avionics bay

The Orbiter has three decks, built one above the other. The commander and pilot control the Orbiter from the top level. This is called the flight deck, and here each of these two crew members has an instrument panel and controls so that either can fly the craft. The mid deck contains the galley, sleep restraints and supplies. The lower deck contains equipment that controls and cleans the air supply to the Orbiter. Food prepared and eaten on the Orbiter is similar to that served on passenger airlines.

USING THE SHUTTLE

The Space Shuttle is designed to do a wide range of jobs in space. The Orbiter has a large payload bay to carry satellites into orbit and bring them back to Earth if necessary. An important tool for this and other jobs is its robot arm, called a Remote Manipulator System (RMS). It is used to take hold of objects in space and place them in the payload bay. It can also carry astronauts back and forth between the Orbiter and another spacecraft. Cameras in the payload bay and attached to the arm enable the astronauts controlling the RMS to watch its movements on television screens in the Orbiter.

For scientific research, the European Space Agency designed a laboratory called Spacelab that fits inside the payload bay. Spacelab is built from a series of units, or modules. This enables it to be changed according to the work planned for each flight. Spacelab is operated by scientist-astronauts called payload specialists.

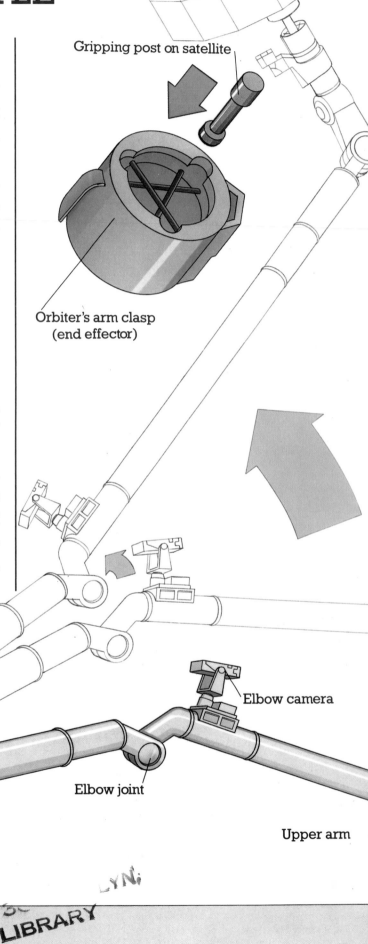

Gripping post on satellite

Orbiter's arm clasp (end effector)

Elbow camera

Shoulder joint

Elbow joint

Lower arm

Upper arm

Attachment to Orbiter

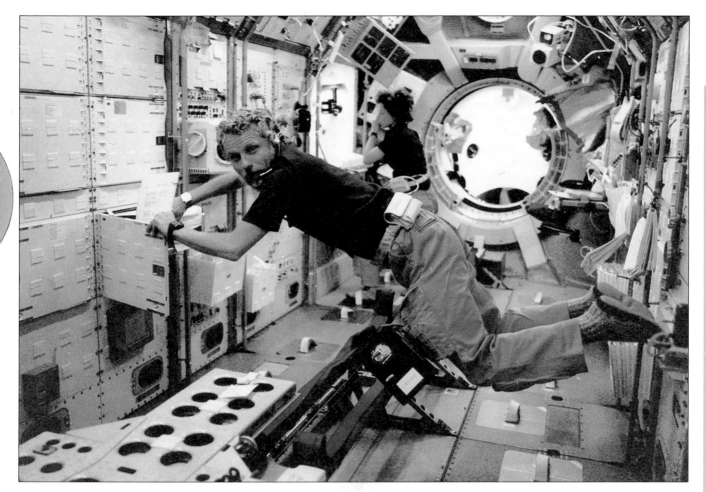

Spacelab-1 was carried on board the ninth Space Shuttle flight in November 1983.

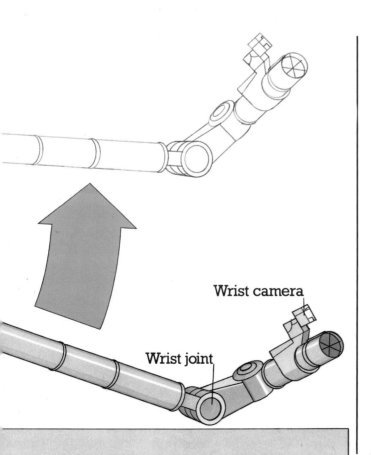

Wrist camera

Wrist joint

The Orbiter's robot arm is 15 m (49 ft) in length and 38 cm (15 in) in diameter. One end is attached to the payload bay. The rest of it can be moved around by electric motors in its joints. It has shoulder, elbow and wrist joints like a human arm. Instead of a hand, it has a device called an end effector. The astronaut controlling the arm uses this to grasp a specially shaped post fitted to satellites and cargo units. Inside the end effector are three crossed wires that can be pulled in to grip the post. With no gravity, heavy loads can be easily moved; a typical satellite carried and launched by the Orbiter weights several tonnes. Some astronauts, known as mission specialists, are trained to control the arm. The RMS is the most advanced robot arm to be used in space, or on Earth. It cost some $25 million to design and build.

17

AT WORK IN SPACE

Astronauts may have to work outside the Orbiter. To do this, they must put on a protective spacesuit and backpack. The backpack contains enough oxygen to breathe for 6 hours in space. Before putting the suit on, the astronaut breathes through a face-mask for a time to change gradually from the Orbiter's oxygen-nitrogen atmosphere to the suit's pure oxygen supply. Water pumped through tubes woven into an undergarment keeps the astronaut cool. With the spacesuit on, the astronaut can move around inside the Orbiter's payload bay.

A Manned Maneuvering Unit (MMU) stored in the payload bay enables astronauts to move away from the Orbiter. The astronaut flies the MMU by firing its nitrogen gas-jets. An automatic control system, the autopilot, helps to keep the MMU in position. This saves the astronaut from having to make continual corrections with the gas-jets.

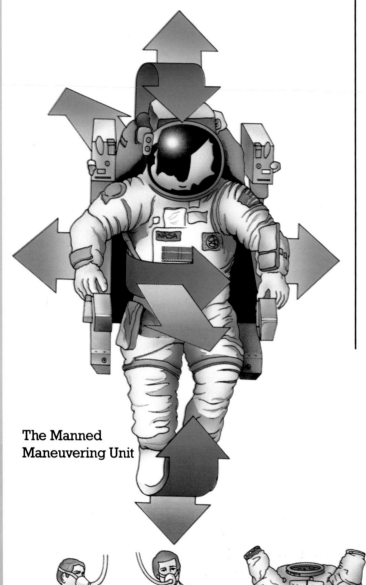

The Manned Maneuvering Unit

The Manned Maneuvering Unit was designed for NASA by the American aerospace company Martin Marietta. Two MMUs were built and they were used for the first time on Space Shuttle flight 41-B in February 1984.

1   2   3   4   5

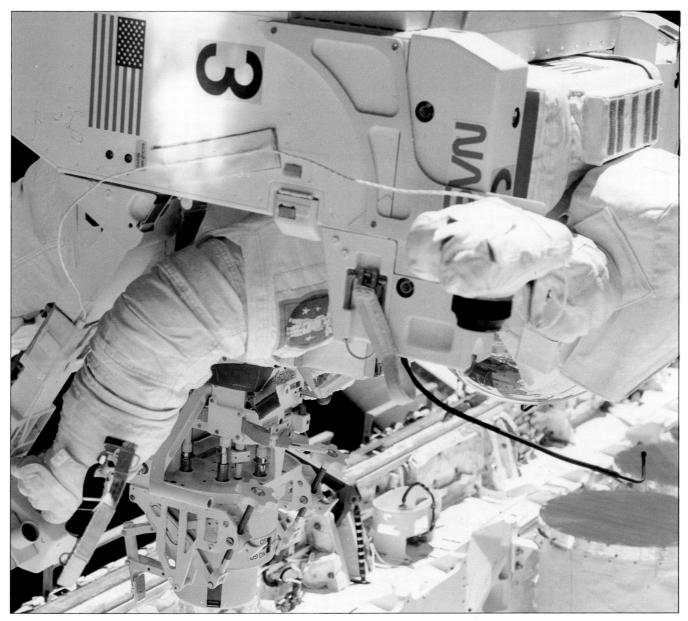

An astronaut uses the MMU to work in space away from the Orbiter

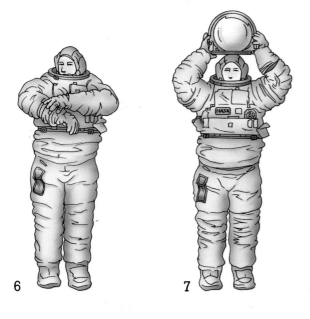

6   7

To put on a spacesuit an astronaut wearing an undergarment (1) pulls on the spacesuit legs first (2). Then the rigid aluminum body section is put on (3) and the two halves of the suit are connected (4). Next comes a headset, known as a "Snoopy Cap" (5). It contains headphones and a microphone for communications. Finally, gloves (6) and a helmet (7) are added. It takes 5 minutes to put on the spacesuit, which is reusable for up to 15 years. In space, the suit allows the astronaut to travel backward, forward, sideways, up and down, and to tilt and roll around.

PAYLOADS

During a Space Shuttle flight it is important that the mission controllers on the ground know exactly where the Space Shuttle is, what it is doing and how the crew are feeling. They do this partly by talking to the crew by radio and partly by receiving data sent to Earth from sensors inside the Shuttle. The information is received by ground stations all over the world.

Since Shuttle flights began in 1981, NASA has been building a network of satellites to replace many of its ground stations. The first of these Tracking and Data Relay Satellites (TDRS-1) was launched by the Shuttle in 1983. TDRS-2 was destroyed with the Orbiter Challenger in 1986. TDRS-3 was put into space by the Shuttle in 1988.

Some of the Shuttle's payloads are scientific instruments. One of the biggest and most important is the Hubble Space Telescope. Above the Earth's atmosphere, this will enable astronomers to see further into space than they can with any telescope on Earth. It will radio its observations to Earth via the TDRS network.

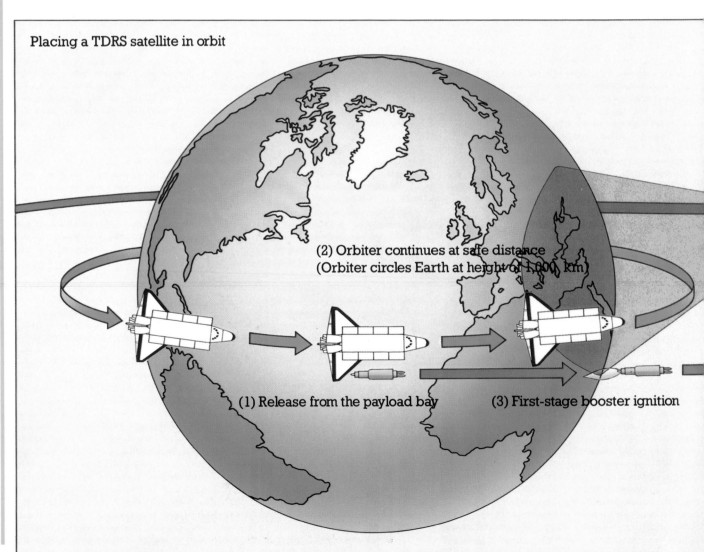

Placing a TDRS satellite in orbit

(1) Release from the payload bay

(2) Orbiter continues at safe distance (Orbiter circles Earth at height of 1,000 km)

(3) First-stage booster ignition

A communications satellite spins around and out of the Orbiter

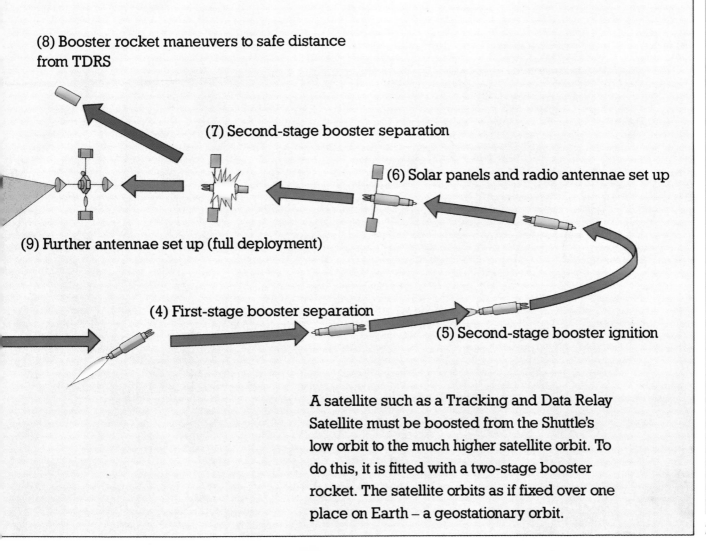

(8) Booster rocket maneuvers to safe distance from TDRS

(7) Second-stage booster separation

(6) Solar panels and radio antennae set up

(9) Further antennae set up (full deployment)

(4) First-stage booster separation

(5) Second-stage booster ignition

A satellite such as a Tracking and Data Relay Satellite must be boosted from the Shuttle's low orbit to the much higher satellite orbit. To do this, it is fitted with a two-stage booster rocket. The satellite orbits as if fixed over one place on Earth – a geostationary orbit.

RE-ENTRY

To begin the Shuttle Obiter's return to Earth, the thrusters are fired to turn the craft around to fly tail first. Then its manouvering engines are fired to slow it down and bring it out of orbit. The craft curves gently downward.

Flying nose-first again, the Orbiter enters the thinnest layers of air 140 km (87 mi) above the Earth. At a height of 130 km (81 mi), the air is thick enough to begin to slow the Orbiter and heat its outer surface. The craft is covered with tiles to protect it from the intense heat. At a height of 70 km (44 mi) the Orbiter is so hot that the air around it becomes disturbed. Radio waves cannot get through this layer of hot air, making all radio communications with the Orbiter impossible for 12 minutes until it slows to about 13,300 km/h (8,200 mph) at a height of 55 km (34 mi).

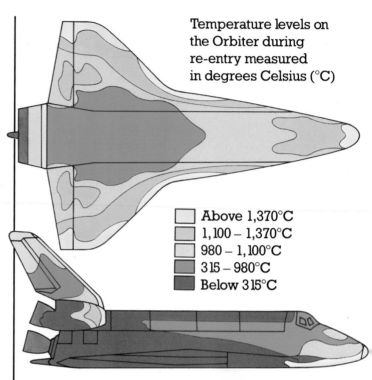

Temperature levels on the Orbiter during re-entry measured in degrees Celsius (°C)

☐	Above 1,370°C
☐	1,100 – 1,370°C
☐	980 – 1,100°C
☐	315 – 980°C
☐	Below 315°C

During re-entry, the hottest parts of the Orbiter reach more than 1,500°C. By comparison, water boils at 100°C and aluminum metal melts at 662°C.

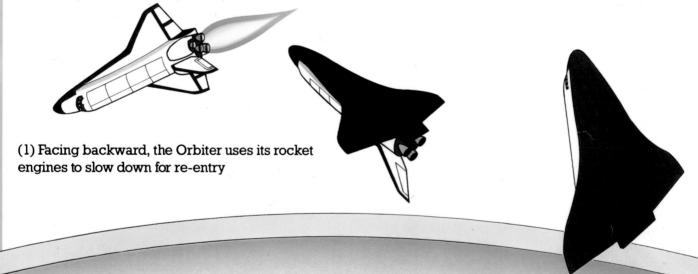

(1) Facing backward, the Orbiter uses its rocket engines to slow down for re-entry

(2) The Orbiter starts to flip over to assume the correct angle

Some 32,000 protective tiles being glued and stuck on to the Orbiter

As the Orbiter begins to descend through the Earth's atmosphere, the crew-members, who were weightless in orbit, begin to feel the effects of gravity pulling them down again. In space there is no air to carry sounds. There is silence outside the spacecraft. On re-entry, the first sound the crew hears from outside the Orbiter is the roar of air rushing past.

(3) Once it is flying at the correct angle, it continues to fall toward the atmosphere

(4) The Orbiter's tiles absorb the heat as it passes through the critical stage of re-entry

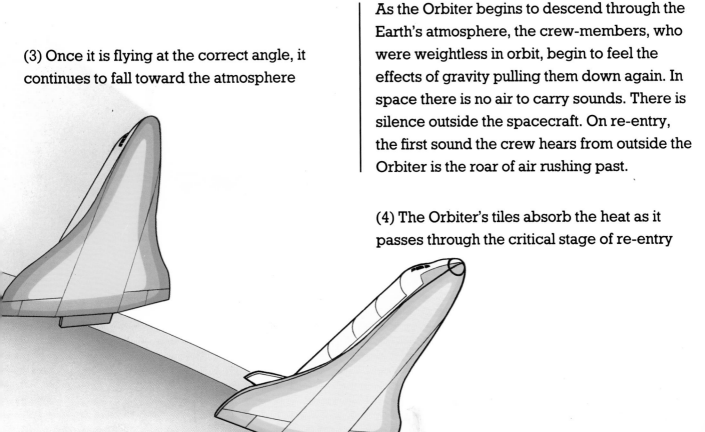

LANDING

After re-entry, air resistance continues to slow the Orbiter. Its rocket engines have run out of fuel and so the craft can only glide down to a landing. It must approach the runway correctly the first time because it has no power to fly around and try again.

Below about 90 km (56 mi) above the Earth, the air becomes thick enough to allow the Orbiter to maneuver by using its rudder and elevons like an airplane. The Orbiter descends along a flight path, the glideslope, which is very steep. A passenger airliner comes in to land on a glideslope with an angle of 2 to 3° (degrees). The Orbiter glides down at 22°. At 500 m (1,600 ft) above the ground and 3 km (2 mi) from the runway, the Orbiter's glideslope is reduced to only 1.5° by a maneuver called flaring.

The Orbiter lands at a speed of 350km/h (210 mph). The main (rear) wheels touch the ground first and then the nose is gently lowered until the nose wheel also touches the ground. Brakes then bring the Orbiter to rest within about 2.5 km (1.5 mi). The specially built Space Shuttle runway at the Kennedy Space Center is 4.5 km (2.7 mi) long.

(1) The Orbiter comes out of re-entry and begins to slow down

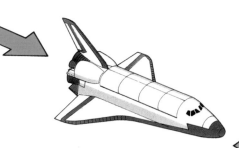

(2) It glides down as it has no fuel left in its engines

(6) When the Orbiter comes to a halt, the crew cannot leave for several minutes because of the heat and the danger from any poisonous or explosive fuel that may be left in the engines

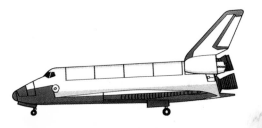

(5) The Orbiter uses its split rudder air-brake to help it slow down

The Shuttle lands safely on an airbase runway

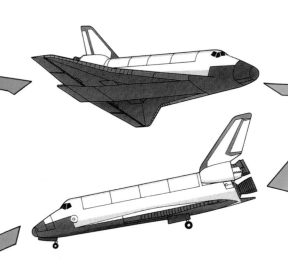

(3) The Orbiter may have to maneuver to land at certain runways

(4) A few feet from the ground the undercarriage is lowered

As the Orbiter has no engine power after re-entry, the place where it is to land must be decided even before it fires its engines to leave orbit. From that moment on, the Shuttle cannot change to another landing site. Below about 4km (2.5 mi), a radio system known as a microwave scanning beam landing system guides the Orbiter down to a safe landing.

THE SOVIET SHUTTLE

Apart from the United States, the only other country that has built and flown a shuttle is the Soviet Union. The Soviet Space Transportation System is called Vozdushno-Kosmichekiy Korabl (VKK), which is Russian for Air Spacecraft. It looks similar to the American shuttle, but there are differences.

The greatest difference between the two shuttles is that the Soviet Orbiter has maneuvering engines and thrusters but no main engines. Instead, powerful engines are fitted to a large launching rocket, the Energia (Energy), to which the orbiter is linked. Extra thrust is provided by four liquid-fueled booster rockets. The Energia rocket returns to Earth by parachute and is used again, unlike the American shuttle's external fuel tank, which is destroyed after its fuel has been used up. This is to recover the very expensive engines.

The Soviet Union's first shuttle flight took place on November 15, 1988. The orbiter was called Buran, which is Russian for Snowstorm. Another orbiter, Ptichka (Birdie), has been built and others are expected in the future.

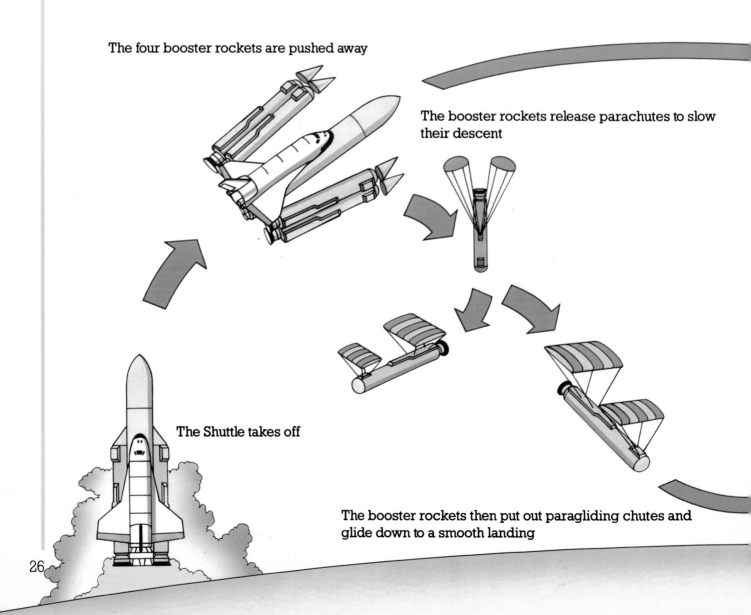

The four booster rockets are pushed away

The booster rockets release parachutes to slow their descent

The Shuttle takes off

The booster rockets then put out paragliding chutes and glide down to a smooth landing

The Soviet Orbiter, Buran, is carried towards its launch site: Buran lands safely

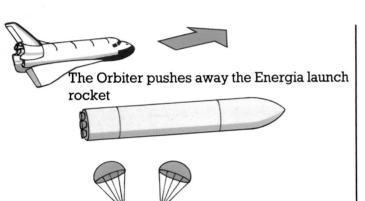

The Orbiter pushes away the Energia launch rocket

A typical Soviet Shuttle flight looks similar to an American Shuttle mission. The Shuttle takes off like a rocket. After it has completed its work in space, the Orbiter lands on a runway like an airplane. The first Soviet Shuttle had no crew. The whole test flight, from launch to landing, was controlled by the Soviet ground station and by the Orbiter's on-board computers.

The rocket is slowed down by primary parachutes

The rocket then divides into three parts, each with its own parachute and air cushions

The Orbiter glides down to Earth in the same way as the American Orbiter does

27

HISTORY OF THE SHUTTLE

Engineers began to think about reusable space shuttles in the 1950s. Many of their early designs were for a two-part craft. The first part was a rocket-powered booster. This provided most of the thrust for take-off. The second part, the Orbiter, was attached to its back. When the booster lifted the Orbiter high enough and fast enough, the Orbiter would separate from it and carry on into orbit. The Bomi, from Bell Aircraft of the United States, was typical of this two-part design. However, none of these craft were built because of the cost and engineering problems.

During the late 1950s and 1960s, the United States built and tested a series of experimental aircraft. Their test flights provided valuable information about flying rockets with wings in the upper layers of the atmosphere. But these craft could not re-enter the atmosphere from space because they would become too hot and burn up. Another type of test craft called a lifting body was developed to research this problem.

The X-15 winged rocket in flight

A series of triangular (delta) shaped lifting bodies were tested. They were launched by being dropped from beneath the wing of a bomber aircraft. The results of these test flights showed that the re-entry problems could be solved.

In 1970 the National Aeronautics and Space Administration (NASA) began a study of the engineering problems of building a reusable Space Shuttle. Different types of craft were studied, ranging from a fully reusable manned booster and Orbiter to a manned Orbiter with add-on booster rockets. The project proved to be very costly. To save money, the Orbiter was made smaller by taking out its main fuel tanks and mounting them separately. The manned booster was replaced by two solid-fueled booster rockets attached to the fuel tank. Studies showed that the Orbiter could glide down to a landing on its own, so the jet engines it was to use for this were taken out. Finally, in 1972, President Richard Nixon announced that NASA was to go ahead and build the Space Shuttle.

An early design for the U.S. Shuttle

U.S. AIR FORCE

The first U.S. Orbiter, Enterprise

Five Orbiters were built. They were Enterprise, Columbia, Challenger, Discovery and Atlantis. Enterprise was only intended for test flights within the atmosphere. It has never flown in space. Columbia was the first to fly in space, in April 1981. Challenger was destroyed in an accident in 1986, killing its crew of seven. Following this, the whole Space Shuttle design was examined and many improvements were made. Shuttle missions resumed with the successful flight of Discovery in September 1988.

The U.S. Challenger explodes in mid-air

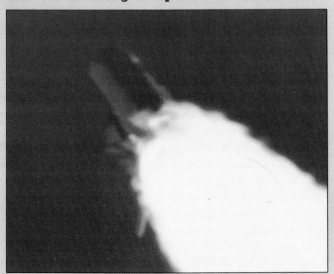

FACTS AND FIGURES

The world's most powerful rocket is the Energia launcher used by the Soviet Union to lift heavy loads such as its Space Shuttle. It measures 60 m (197 ft) in height, has a maximum diameter of 16 m (52 ft), weighs 2,000 tons and produces a thrust of 4,000 tonnes. It can place a satellite of 130 tons in Earth orbit. Energia was launched first in May 1987.

The largest crew carried on a single space mission was the crew of eight carried in the Challenger Orbiter of Shuttle flight 61-A, the 22nd Shuttle flight, on October 30th 1985. The mission was commanded by Frank Hartsfield and lasted for 7 days.

Of more than 200 people who have traveled in space, the oldest was Karl Henize who was a mission specialist on Shuttle flight 51-F in July 1985. He was then 58 years old.

The worst accident during a spaceflight was the destruction of the U.S. Challenger Orbiter by an explosion 73 seconds after take-off in January 1986. The seven crew members were all killed instantly.

Shuttle astronaut John Young has made more spaceflights than anyone else. At the end of the ninth Shuttle flight in 1983, he had made six flights and spent a total of 34 days 42 minutes and 13 seconds in space.

GLOSSARY

altitude
Height above the Earth's surface.

astronaut
A person trained to fly a spacecraft.

booster rocket
A rocket used to provide extra thrust.

elevon
A movable flap on each of the Orbiter's wings, used to maneuver the craft in the atmosphere. It acts like the two types of airplane flaps, an elevator and an aileron.

geostationary/geosynchronous
An orbit 36,000 km (22,000 mi) above the Earth's equator. A satellite in this orbit keeps pace with the Earth as it spins around and appears to hang over the same spot on the Earth all the time.

glideslope
The flight path angle the Orbiter follows when it is landing.

gravity
The force of attraction between two large objects. The "pull" of the Earth's force of gravity must be overcome to launch the Shuttle into space.

gyroscope
A spinning wheel used in navigation and guidance systems to detect movement of a craft.

lox
Liquid oxygen.

mission specialist
A member of the Space Shuttle crew trained to supervise the payload; to timetable experiments; to carry out some experiments; and, if necessary, to assist the payload specialist.

NASA
The National Aeronautics and Space Administration, the United States' space agency.

O-ring
A rubbery ring that helps stop gases leaking through a joint between metal parts – especially in the joints of the Shuttle's Solid Rocket Boosters.

orbit
The flight path of a spacecraft or satellite as it circles the Earth.

orbital maneuvering system
Rocket engines used to move the Shuttle Orbiter around while it is in space.

Orbiter
The only part of the Space Shuttle that travels into orbit and returns to Earth.

payload
The Space Shuttle's cargo of satellites or scientific experiments.

payload specialist
A member of the Shuttle crew trained to operate the payload.

pitch
A nose-up or nose-down movement.

roll
Motion that rocks a spacecraft to the left or to the right.

rudder
A flap in the vertical stabilizer used to steer the Orbiter to the left or right as it comes in to land.

solid rocket booster
A solid-fueled rocket that provides extra thrust to help the Space Shuttle take off.

space telescope
The Hubble Space Telescope, named after the U.S. astronomer Edwin Hubble, was specially designed to be launched by the Space Shuttle. It will enable astronomers on Earth to see further into the universe than ever before.

TDRS
Tracking and Data Relay Satellite. A satellite used to monitor the Space Shuttle and the satellites it launches, and to relay Shuttle voice and data communications to ground stations.

thrust
The pushing force produced by a rocket engine.

thruster
A tiny rocket motor used to make small adjustments to a spacecraft's position.

yaw
Turning movements to the left or right, like a car turning around a corner.

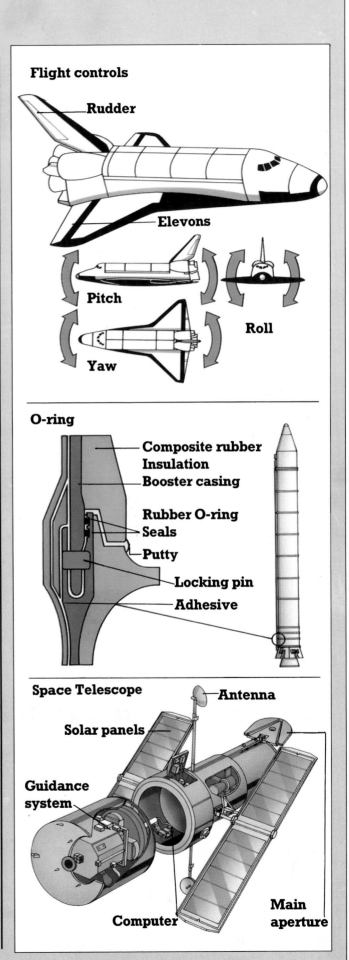

Flight controls
- Rudder
- Elevons
- Pitch
- Yaw
- Roll

O-ring
- Composite rubber
- Insulation
- Booster casing
- Rubber O-ring
- Seals
- Putty
- Locking pin
- Adhesive

Space Telescope
- Antenna
- Solar panels
- Guidance system
- Computer
- Main aperture

INDEX

Photographic credits
Cover and pages 8 and inset, 14, 19, 23, 25, 28
and 29: NASA via Astro Information Service;
pages 7tl and 27: Associated Press; page 7tr:
Aerospatiale; page 7b: British Aerospace;
pages 10 and 17: NASA / Aladdin Books; page
21: Rockwell Int.; page 27 inset: Novosti.